Costume in Context

The 1940s and 1950s

Jennifer Ruby

B.T. Batsford Ltd, London

Foreword

When studying costume it is important to understand the difference between fashion and costume. Fashion tends to predict the future – that is, what people *will* be wearing – and very fashionable clothes are usually worn only by people wealthy enough to afford them. For example, even today, the clothes that appear in fashionable magazines are not the same as those being worn by the majority of people in the street. Costume, on the other hand, represents what people are actually wearing at a given time, which may be quite different from what is termed 'fashionable' for their day.

Each book in this series is built round a fictitious family. By following the various members, sometimes over several generations – and the people with whom they come into contact – you will be able to see the major fashion developments of the period and compare the clothing and lifestyles of people from all walks of life. You will meet servants, soldiers, street-sellers and beggars as well as the very wealthy, and you will see how their different clothing reflects their particular occupations and circumstances.

Major social changes are mentioned in each period and you will see how clothing is adapted as people's needs and attitudes change. The date list will help you to understand more fully how historical events affect the clothes that people wear.

Many of the drawings in these books have been taken from contemporary paintings. During the course of your work perhaps you could visit some museums and art galleries yourself in order to learn more about the costumes of the period you are studying from the artists who painted at that time.

c. 1947

This book is for my mother, who wore the clothes and shared her memories.

Acknowledgments

The sources for the illustrations have often been contemporary drawings and prints. I would like to acknowledge in particular: Frontispiece, after Dereta fashion plate; page 10, after R. Whistler; page 12, after Marshall and Snelgrove Catalogue; page 19, after Windrow and Hook; page 27 (centre), after E. Dunbar; page 46, after Charles Wood. Colour plate 'The Visit' after a *Vogue* advertisement.

© Jennifer Ruby 1989
First published 1989
Reprinted 1993, 1995

Typeset by Tek-Art Ltd, Kent
and printed and bound in Great Britain
by The Bath Press, Bath
for the publishers
B.T. Batsford Ltd
4 Fitzhardinge Street
London W1H 0AH

ISBN 0 7134 6016 4

Contents

c. 1945

Date List

1939 Declaration of war with Germany.
A 'military look' to women clothes; lounge suits are popular with men.

1940 The Germans arrive in Paris and close down the French fashion houses. The USA is forced to look to its own resources for fashion inspiration rather than take the lead from Europe.

1941 Clothes rationing is introduced. Clothes must now last for years. 'Make do and mend' becomes a popular war-time slogan.
The production of silk stockings is banned.
John Whinfield invents Terylene which is to revolutionize men's trousers.
Nylon is produced in Britain for the first time.
The National Service Act makes unmarried women and childless widows (aged 18-25) liable for military service.
Women are wearing trousers more and more as they are practical and convenient.

1942 The Incorporated Society of London Fashion Designers is formed.
The Utility Scheme is introduced. Individuality in fashion is now lost, women try to ring the changes with unusual headgear (hats are not rationed).
USA enters the war.

1944 Paris is liberated.

1945 The war ends. Demobilization begins.

1945-50 Various Acts of Parliament create the Welfare State.

1946 The 'Britain Can Make It' exhibition is staged at the Victoria and Albert Museum.
Many British fashion designs are exhibited, but for export only.

1947 Christian Dior launches his New Look to the fashion world.

1949 Enough yarn to make 50 million pairs of nylon stockings is produced by Britain's nylon spinners.

1950 The first micro-groove plastic disc appears in the USA. The rise of 'pop' music.

1954 Wartime restrictions have finally disappeared and many large department stores take the opportunity to expand providing better variety and availability of good quality clothes.
The 'Young Revolution' is in full swing. Teenagers are now demanding their own style of clothes. Casual wear is now becoming more popular. Blue jeans have come to stay.

1955 Mary Quant opens her first boutique in the Kings Road, London. She is a young designer who responds to the needs of young people.

1960 There is more freedom of choice, and a greater prosperity. Clothes are easily available and there is a greater variety of styles and fabrics than ever before.

Introduction

The 20 years covered by this book (1940-1960) were a time of enormous upheaval and change. In 1940 Britain was in the grip of World War II, enduring restrictions, rationing and hardship, but by 1960 the country was entering a new age of freedom and prosperity the like of which it had never seen before.

During the war years life in Britain became steadily more drab and austere. Clothes rationing was introduced in 1941, so clothes had to last for years. The Utility Scheme of 1942, designed to restrict the amount of material used in the manufacture of clothing, provided reasonably priced, good quality garments but the restriction on styles meant that individuality in dress was lost. This, coupled with the closure of the Paris fashion houses during the German occupation, made it seem as if fashion had come to a standstill. Women's skirts were fairly short, their waists small and their shoulders squared giving a military look to their figures. In order to save on material, men's suits were cut with single-breasted jackets and had no pocket flaps and trousers were without turnups. In spite of the restrictions however, people rallied to the cause and there was a kind of fashionable patriotic austerity. 'Make Do and Mend' was a popular war-time slogan and everyone stretched their imaginations to make clothes last longer and make new garments from old ones.

c. 1950

As in World War I, women found themselves suddenly left without men and therefore they took on many men's jobs, and became, for example, ambulance drivers, wardens, mechanics and window cleaners. Thousands more joined the armed forces as auxiliaries and proved themselves invaluable to the war effort. Slacks and pullovers became popular war-time wear for many women because they were both practical for work and warm during the night time air raids. Women enjoyed the freedom of wearing trousers and they have remained popular ever since.

It is hard for us now, in a time of relative plenty, to imagine life in England during World War II. There were black-outs and air raids, food and clothing were strictly rationed, petrol was very scarce and television had been closed down. The radio was the principal means of diversion and there was a feeling of contraction as people were restricted in their movements, in the food they ate and the clothes they wore so it was quite understandable that when the war ended the pendulum swung the other way. The great French fashion houses reopened after the liberation of Paris and in 1947 Christian Dior, a French couturier, launched his 'New Look' to the fashion world. Women loved the narrow shoulders, shapely bustline and long flowing skirts of his designs because they represented everything that had been lacking during the war years. There was great excitement and intense activity in the fashion world and each year new designs were launched to a hungry market. The style in men's clothes remained very much the same except that with the gradual lifting of restrictions manufacturers were able to use more material and suits returned to their prewar styles.

Mary Quant
Design, 1958

Teddy Boy,
1957

sports jacket,
1949

utility fashion
1945

suit,
1954

suit,
1953

1945

1943

1959

black crêpe
afternoon dress,
1947

1951

1946

6

By 1950 things were almost back to normal. There was a mood of optimism, things were expanding and life was becoming easier. The Welfare State, created in 1945-50, provided better care for people; production was good, generating more jobs and more money which in turn lead to greater freedom. The fashion look of the 1950s was a sophisticated one. Women wanted to look perfectly groomed with matching accessories and lovely make-up and 'beauty' became big business now that wartime cosmetic shortages were over.

As fashion had come to a virtual standstill in Paris during the war, America had been forced to look to its own resources for inspiration rather than take the lead from Europe as it had done previously. The look that developed in the USA was practical rather than romantic, colourful and more casual than in Europe. After the war the American 'style' became popular in the UK. Practical shirtwaister dresses, sweaters, shorts and blue jeans were fashionable, creating a more relaxed and sporty look.

One of the most interesting features of the 1950s was the young revolution. Many more young people were now economically independent and had greater freedom than ever before. They wanted their own styles and their own lives and no longer wished to copy their parents. This led to new teenage styles, two popular ones being the 'student' look – a sweater and slacks – and the Teddy boy image. Department stores began opening up teenage boutiques to cater for this new market and in 1955 Mary Quant opened her first boutique on London's Kings Road. She was a young designer responding to the needs of youth and provided smart and relatively inexpensive clothes that were both original and colourful and these soon became immensely popular.

During the 1940s and 1950s the ready-to-wear industries were growing ever stronger. There were more and more man-made fibres and good quality fashionable clothes were produced on a large scale for expanding department stores like Marks and Spencer. This meant that stylish clothes were readily available and affordable for more people. These changes affected children's clothing too. The department stores catered for their needs and companies like Ladybird were expanding rapidly and providing good quality clothes that were practical for young energetic lives.

From 1940 to 1960 Britain moved from austerity to prosperity. Restrictions, rationing and sacrifice gradually gave way to freedom, plenty and affluence. The war had been a great leveller in that no one, whether rich or poor, had been untouched by it and after it was over the new prosperity meant that good quality material things were within the reach of more people. In this book you will meet characters from all walks of life and in different circumstances. Think about some of the points mentioned above and see how the changes taking place in society affect the clothes they wear.

c. 1951

A Lawyer, c. 1940

It is 1940 and Britain is in the grip of World War II. This is Richard Somerville who is a wealthy lawyer. He and his family live in London but since the outbreak of the war they have been spending more time at their country home away from the danger of the air raids.

On the right Richard is wearing a double-breasted grey flannel suit with pinstripes, a soft cotton shirt and a black tie. His hair is short and well brushed and he likes to put Brilliantine on it to keep the style in place.

On the opposite page you can see other items from his extensive wardrobe. When in London, Richard might wear a long overcoat over his suit when going to work and he would also wear smart shirts and ties. When in the country however, he tends to wear more informal clothes but he does have separate outfits for each of his favourite pursuits of shooting, golf and riding. The riding outfit is shown and consists of a hacking jacket, jodpurs, a soft felt hat and a shirt with a button-down collar.

Government controls on clothing gradually became tighter during the war years. Due to a shortage of material the amount used in the manufacture of garments was strictly controlled which meant that men's waistcoats, trouser turnups and double shirt cuffs gradually disappeared and their shirt tails became shorter.

woollen vest
and pants

riding
outfit

long woollen
overcoat

plain shirt
with collar
and pocket

fancy striped
pyjamas

striped cotton
shirt, detachable
collar

tweed country hat

top hat for formal wear

The Lawyer's Wife, c. 1940

Here is Richard's wife Audrey sitting in the garden of their country home. She is wearing a light collarless coat with padded shoulders and a waist belt, a dark, high-necked dress and court shoes. She has her hair parted in the centre and softly waved.

Other items from her wardrobe are pictured on the opposite page. The fashionable look is a square-shouldered, almost military style and skirts are quite short. Due to the war, fabric supplies are becoming scarce and good accessories more difficult to find. However, Audrey can afford to pay more for good quality clothes so her wardrobe has not yet suffered.

She owns a large collection of dresses, suits, coats and hats and many pairs of shoes. When in London it is necessary to carry a gas mask at all times due to the threat of air raids. As they are rather ugly, Audrey carries hers in a smart bag when she is out for the evening.

Like many women, Audrey enjoys wearing make-up. She uses eyeshadows, mascaras for tinting her eyelashes and deep red lipsticks and nail varnishes.

dress with
mock bolero
fronts applied
to bodice

evening gas mask bag,
made of cotton, embroidered
in rayon, short carrying
handles

long
housecoat
with cross-over
bodice

worsted
dress and
jacket

court shoe, top
decorated with
studs

high front
lace shoe

black suede
dress shoe

platform
sandal

crêpe dress, trimmed with
gold embroidery

The Lawyer's Children, c. 1940

Here are the Somervilles' children, Catherine, Jane, James and Elizabeth. They are all together in the garden of their parents' country house and are wearing practical, woollen clothes which are both warm and comfortable.

Jane and James (left) are twins and are nine years old. Jane is wearing a blue knitted jersey with a collar, a colourful knitted beret and a light woollen skirt. James has on a knitted slipover, a short-sleeved cotton shirt and short flannel trousers. Elizabeth is five. She is wearing a matching outfit in royal blue which consists of a beret, coat and tights.

Catherine is 15 and is on holiday from her boarding school. On the opposite page she is wearing a crochet hat with a peak and a knitted cardigan suit which has the fashionable square-shouldered look.

Trousers had been worn by some women for informal occasions since the 1920s but the fashion did not become widespread until World War II when they proved to be both practical and warm. Catherine loves to wear them and in the picture below she has on a corduroy pair which have wide legs and turned-up hems. She is also wearing a short knitted Shetland wool sweater and practical sporty shoes which have thick crêpe rubber soles. Catherine likes to keep up with the fashions even though it is war time. She wears her hair in the latest styles and often experiments with bright lipsticks and nail varnishes.

The Somerville children are very lucky that their parents have a country home as it enables the family to stay together in spite of the war. Many children who lived in London and other large cities were evacuated to the country away from the threat of air raids. This meant that they had to leave their parents and live with a strange family, sometimes for the duration of the war. How do you think this would have felt?

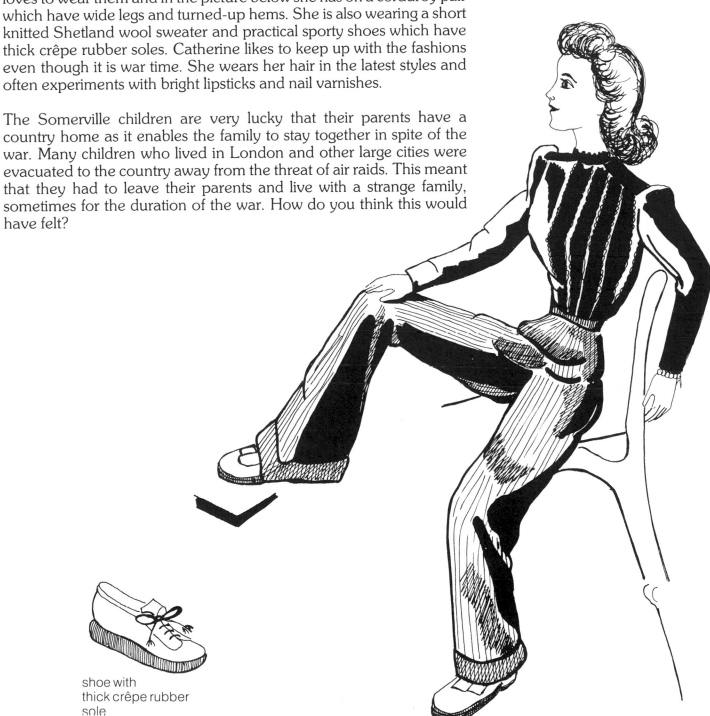

shoe with
thick crêpe rubber
sole

Practical Clothes, c. 1940

War-time conditions, with the growing scarcity of good clothes and materials and the constant threat of air raids day and night, meant that women needed practical, hard-wearing clothes in their wardrobes.

Mary Adams does a part-time cleaning job at the Somervilles' London home. She is on her way to work and is wearing a warm woollen coat over a skirt and blouse, a floral headscarf and crêpe-soled shoes. In her bag she is carrying her cleaning apron.

Mary is talking to her daughter Susan who is a typist in a bank nearby. Susan is wearing a knitted jumper and matching cardigan, a checked tweed skirt with inverted pleats and she has a scarf tied, turban fashion, over her curls. Even though her clothes are practical she still displays the fashionable look of square shoulders, with a slim waist and hips.

On this page Susan is talking to her friend Joan who also works at the bank. Susan is wearing an all-in-one shelter (or siren) suit, which is a combined hooded jacket and trousers in woollen cloth. It is comfortable, warm and easy to slip into for night-time visits to the air raid shelter.

Joan is wearing a button-through cotton dress and low heeled shoes.

The war has brought great unhappiness to Mary Adams as it has fragmented her family. Her husband is serving in the army so she only sees him when he is home on leave and her three youngest children are soon to be evacuated with their school away from the dangers of London.

Evacuee Children, c. 1940

Mr Humphries is the headmaster of a small junior school in London. Today he is very sad because his school is closing due to the war and his pupils are being evacuated to the country for safety. They have all arrived this morning clutching their luggage and gas masks and with identity labels around their necks. They will be taken to a village in Norfolk where they will all attend the village school and each child will be allocated a family with whom they will live.

Mr Humphries is wearing a single-breasted lounge suit, a white cotton shirt and a black tie. He is checking off the names of some of his pupils against his list.

Alice, Tom and Alan are Mary's children. She has sent them to school today not knowing when she will see them again. Alice is wearing a woollen coat and hat, a floral print dress, lace-up shoes and white ankle socks. Her brothers are both wearing double-breasted jackets, short trousers, long woollen socks and lace-up shoes.

In another room Mrs Humphries is helping Peter with a new gas mask as his old one was damaged. She is wearing a cotton print overall over her dress.

Peter is wearing a knitted slipover, a short-sleeved cotton shirt, trousers and braces. His mother made his trousers from an old pair of his father's as she could not afford a new pair for him.

In the foreground, two sisters, Shirley and Marcia, anxiously await instructions from their teacher. They are both wearing woollen coats over cotton dresses, white socks and bar shoes. Their parents are worried about them leaving home and going to live in a strange new environment. They have put a label on the girls which reads 'please do not separate' in the hope that Shirley and Marcia will at least have each other when they are allocated their temporary home and 'family'.

Two Soldiers, c. 1940

This is John Adams, Mary's eldest son, who is sixteen. He is in the Local Defence Volunteers which is an army of unpaid, part-time men whose job it is to defend the country in the event of an invasion. The members are either too young or too old to be in the regular army or are engaged in jobs which are thought to be vital to the country and from which they cannot be spared.

At present they have no uniform and wear their ordinary clothes with the addition of a steel helmet and an armlet bearing the letters LDV. Their equipment often consists of anything they can find including broom handles and farm implements, although they do have a few obsolete weapons from World War I at their disposal.

As the LDVs became more organized, they were issued with a proper uniform and better equipment and were known as the Home Guard. See if you can find someone who used to serve in the Home Guard. Interview them and ask them about some of their experiences.

John's father Harry is in France fighting with the British army. In the picture opposite you can see him outside a two-man 'slit trench' which will provide him with shelter from the danger of mortar, artillery and air attack while the troops rest for a while.

Harry is wearing his khaki serge battle dress which has many pockets. In the winter he wears it with extra pullovers and a greatcoat. His steel helmet is covered with a camouflage net which has green and brown hessian strips attached to it. Some of his equipment is also in the picture.

c. 1940

How do you think it would feel to spend a night in a slit trench?

mug

mess tin

torch

jackknife

gas mask

Utility Clothes, 1942

In June 1941, due to all the shortages caused by the war, the government introduced clothes rationing. Everyone was issued with 66 clothes coupons which were to last them for 12 months, although the number had decreased to 36 coupons by the end of the war. A different number of coupons had to be surrendered for different garments and people soon discovered that they did not go very far. For example, a man's overcoat took 16 coupons, a suit 26 and socks 3. A woman's woollen dress took 11, a shirt 7 and a blouse 5.

In addition to this, the Utility Scheme was introduced in 1942, the idea being to limit the amount of cloth used in the making of garments. A committee of designers got together and produced standard patterns for dresses, suits and coats which were simple and used minimum amounts of material. For example, men's jackets were single-breasted, had no more than three pockets, no buttons on the cuffs and the seam allowances were skimpy. All Utility clothes carried the label ❝❝41.

This is Henry, Audrey Somerville's brother, who runs a small textile business in the north of England. He and his wife Olivia are spending a few days with the Somervilles. Henry is wearing a Utility suit. The trousers have no turnups and the jacket does not have a breast pocket or buttoned cuffs. His waistcoat has only two pockets.

On the opposite page, Olivia is wearing a Utility suit in wool. The short military-style jacket is light blue, the skirt is dark blue and she is wearing a red blouse and matching red hat. Other examples of Utility styles are shown in the background.

Utility clothes were not unattractive but they were restrictive and it was difficult for a woman to be original. Many ladies tried to ring the changes by wearing different and attractive hats (which were not rationed), and bright lipsticks and nail varnishes.

What do you think people's reactions would be today if the government imposed these kind of restrictions?

plain woollen dress

hats to brighten up an outfit

box coat

Utility suit

Make Do and Mend, 1942

As clothing was so scarce, many women used their initiative to make new garments or to alter old, pre-war ones. Magazines were full of ideas on how to do this and the government encouraged people with the slogan 'Make Do and Mend'. Old curtains could be turned into skirts, two knitted dishcloths could be made into a jumper, old evening dresses converted into slacks and old dresses into overalls and aprons. Many shops offered a service of remodelling and repair of clothes to their customers.

Here is Susan Adams, who is quite a good needlewoman. She is wearing a cotton dress that she has made herself. It has gauging at the shoulders and at the top of the skirt front panel. She is also wearing a turban hat decorated with an artificial flower.

On the opposite page Susan is wearing another dress that she has made from two old ones and you can also see a bolero suit which has been made from an old coat. Stockings are scarce and expensive on coupons so when Susan goes dancing she paints a line down the backs of her legs so that it looks as though she is wearing seamed stockings!

Children's clothing was particularly difficult during the war years as they grew out of their clothes so quickly and there was never enough money or coupons to replace them. Susan has helped her mother by making various garments for Alice, Tom and Alan and sending them to Norfolk where they are living on a farm. On the right Alice is wearing a pinafore that Susan has made from an old cotton sheet.

Look around your home. Can you find any items that you could usefully convert into clothing if you had to? What would it be like to 'make do and mend'?

government poster to encourage saving in the home

MAKE-DO AND MEND

says Mrs. Sew-and-Sew

dress made from two old ones

bolero suit made from old coat

pinafore overdress

Women in Uniform, c. 1943

During World War II many women joined the armed forces as auxiliaries. Their contribution to the war effort was invaluable as they freed men for active service abroad while they manned operations at home. They worked in many different fields, including communications, catering and maintenance.

Here is Catherine Somerville who is now 18 and has joined the Auxiliary Territorial Service (ATS), the women's branch of the army. She is wearing her khaki uniform which consists of a belted, pocketed army jacket, a mid-calf skirt, a shirt, a tie and a soft-crowned peaked cap. She has also been issued with Service underwear which includes bras, cream-coloured cotton and wool knickers, vests and lisle stockings. In addition she has been given what many recruits laughingly refer to as 'passion killers'. These are over-knickers of artificial silk which are knee-length and khaki coloured. Catherine has been told that she will not be able to wear her hair in this loose style, instead she must adopt one of the styles pictured on the right in order to keep her hair neat and tidy.

On the opposite page we see Catherine's cousin Geraldine (Harry and Olivia's daughter), who has joined the Women's Royal Naval Service (WRNS). Her uniform consists of a smart navy suit, a white shirt, a black tie, opaque black stockings and laced shoes.

One of Catherine's friends is in the Woman's Auxiliary Air Force (WAAF) and she is also pictured opposite.

Thousands of women contributed to the war effort without joining the forces. They worked as Air Raid Wardens, Ambulance Drivers, Postmen, Train Drivers, Mechanics and in many other jobs normally done by men. For example, on the far right you can see Mrs Scott who is working as an Air Raid Warden. Her son Peter (whom you met on page 17) is an evacuee and her husband is fighting abroad so she finds the work helps to fill in some of her lonely hours.

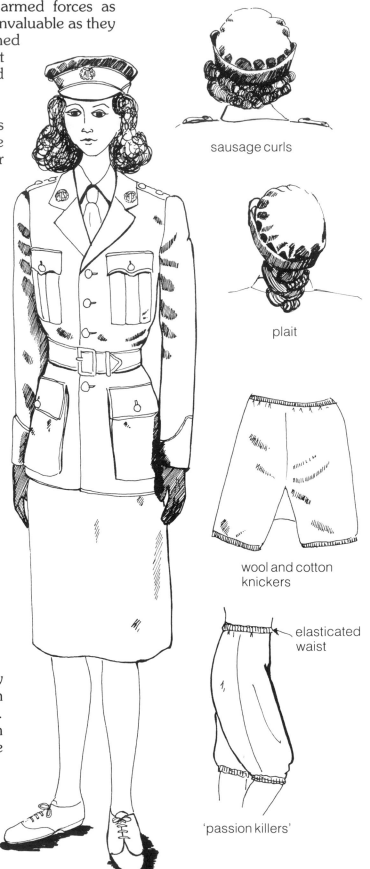

sausage curls

plait

wool and cotton knickers

elasticated waist

'passion killers'

Find out more about the role of women during the war. In particular, find out how the different occupations they followed influenced the clothes that they wore.

WAAF uniform

WRN uniform

Air Raid Warden

The Women's Land Army, c. 1943

During the war farms were short of agricultural workers because so many men had joined the army. Because of this, and the urgent need to supply food to the nation, the Women's Land Army was reformed in 1939. Women joined up in their thousands and made an important contribution to the war effort by undertaking a wide variety of jobs from milking and caring for livestock to driving tractors.

Here is Susan who has left her typing job and joined the WLA with her friend Joan. Susan is wearing the WLA uniform which consists of a brown felt hat, khaki breeches, a shirt and tie, a green jersey, woollen socks and stout shoes. She has also been given an overcoat, overalls and a mackintosh.

Susan is very pleased because she asked if she and Joan could be posted to the farm in Norfolk where her sister and two younger brothers are evacuees. She was granted her request and on the opposite page you can see them in action. In the centre, Susan is wearing overalls over her uniform and a soft, deep-brimmed hat. When operating machinery or doing muddy jobs, the girls often wear dungarees and wellingtons as in the other two pictures.

Farm work is very different from being a typist. The girls find the country very quiet after London but they love the fresh air and are even growing to like some of the animals!

At first many farmers were sceptical that women would be able to do agricultural labouring as well as men. However, the WLA soon proved itself invaluable and received much praise and admiration. The song on the opposite page was written by Victoria Sackville West and was intended to encourage the land girls.

Back to the Land, with its clay and its
    sand,
Its granite and gravel and grit.
You grow barley and wheat,
And potatoes to eat,
To make sure the nation keeps fit.

A Farmer and his Wife, c. 1943

This is Fred Westlake the farmer. He is very pleased to have the help of the WLA on his farm as there is so much work to be done. The war has meant a reduction in imports and as a result more food has to be grown at home. Farmers are being compelled by the government to convert to more efficient agricultural methods and break up any grass fields and sow them with approved crops.

Fred is wearing a trilby hat, a collarless shirt, a pinstripe jacket and waistcoat, woollen breeches and wellington boots. His clothes are quite old, but Fred would not have the time or money for fashionable garments even if there were not a war on.

Fred's wife Edith is in the kitchen. She is wearing a cross-over cotton print overall and matching head-scarf which she has made herself. She also has on a knitted jumper, a black woollen skirt and warm slippers and socks. In the background Susan and Tom are digging in the garden where they are growing vegetables to feed the family. What are they wearing?

Edith and Fred are very pleased with their new 'family'. They both miss their own children who are grown up and have now moved away and they find the evacuees both polite and helpful. Edith is growing very fond of them and will be sad when they eventually return home.

DIG FOR VICTORY

government poster encouraging
people to grow food

An American GI, c. 1943

Large numbers of American servicemen were stationed in Britain during the war. They were known as GIs from the words 'Government Issue' which were stamped on their equipment.

This is Bob, a GI who is stationed at a base near the farm where Susan and Joan work. He is wearing his uniform which consists of a khaki single-breasted tunic with four gilt buttons down the front, breast and side patch pockets with flaps and buttons, and a matching cloth belt, khaki trousers, brown boots and canvas leggings. He is also wearing a helmet and a khaki shirt and tie. Some of his equipment is also shown in the picture.

Dances are often held at the American base. Lorries collect the local girls from nearby towns and take them, with chaperons, to the base.

On the opposite page you can see Joan, who is all ready to go to one of these dances. She has spent some time getting ready and making herself as fashionable as her wartime wardrobe will allow.

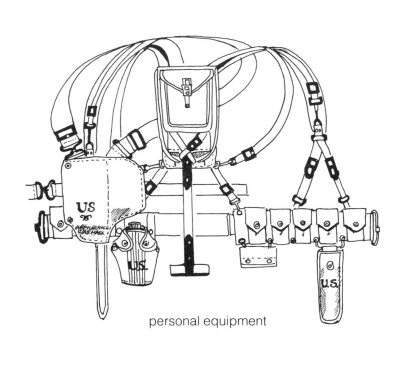

personal equipment

Going to a Dance, c. 1943

Joan is wearing a linen dress with a button-through bodice and flared skirt which has a box pleat in the front. She has her hair in one of the latest styles. To achieve the effect she wanted she set it in pin curls earlier in the evening.

Joan's underwear is pictured on the far right. She is very lucky because she has nylon stockings to wear to the dance. These were a gift from Bob whom she is dating. The GIs often seem to have an endless supply of things that are scarce in England and Joan frequently receives gifts of fruit, chocolate, candy and cigarettes from Bob, making her the envy of her friends!

The GIs are not very popular with the local young men. Why do you think this is?

hair in pincurls

cotton bra and
French knickers

nylons

gifts from the
American base

Demobilization – Men, 1945-6

After the war ended in 1945, many troops had to be disbanded or 'demobilized'. Soldiers were brought back to England and sent to one of 380 dispersal centres where they handed in their army uniforms and received their 'demob' clothes. These consisted of a suit, one shirt, two collars, two pairs of socks, one pair of shoes, one pair of cuff links, a tie and a hat.

Here is Harry Adams who is being fitted for his demob suit which is in dark grey flannel with a white pin-stripe. The jacket is double-breasted with two hip pockets with flaps, a breast pocket, six buttons on the front and three on the cuffs. The trousers will have three pockets and turnups. How does this differ from the suit on page 20?

How do you think it would feel to return to civilian life after fighting in a war? What sort of problems would there be?

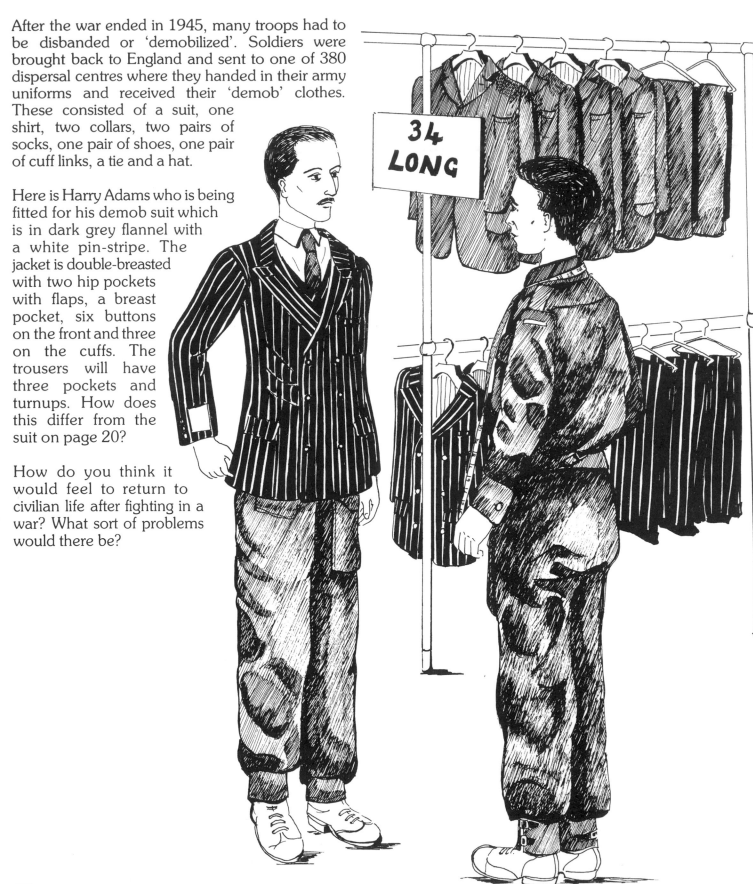

The visit, c. 1940

Summer dresses, c. 1945

Beach wear, c. 1949

Young fashion, c. 1954

N.B. It is dangerous to ride scooters or motorcycles without crash helmets, which are now compulsory.

Fashions, c. 1957

Good neighbours, c. 1954

Rock 'n' Roll, c. 1958

Demobilization – Women, 1945-6

When women were released from active service they were not given a set of clothes because the authorities felt that they would not be able to cope with the whims and fancies of ladies' fashion tastes! Instead they were issued with coupons and cash to buy new clothes for themselves.

Vogue magazine advertised garments like these as being excellent buys for demobilized service women.

When women were demobilized they had to hand in their uniforms but were allowed to keep their underwear, kitbags and shoe brushes.

Imagine that you have just been discharged from service like this. What clothes will you buy for yourself with the money and coupons you have been given? What will be the most essential items?

pill box hat

small hat with bow and net trim

pinafore dress

fitted pin-stripe suit

court shoes

smooth, slim-fitting woollen coat with braid trimming

suede and leather court shoes

shoes with medium heel and bow decoration

Britain Can Make It, 1946

In September 1946 the Council for Industrial Design staged an exhibition at the Victoria and Albert Museum in London. It was called 'Britain Can Make It' and was intended to be a huge advertisement for goods manufactured in Britain. It was hoped that the exhibition would not only boost British exports but also help to raise public morale after the hardship of the war years.

Clothing and accessories were included in the exhibition and a great deal of interest was focused on women's wear. Fifteen top London designers exhibited in the Fashion Hall which was divided into three sections for inexpensive, medium-priced and designer clothes. Thousands of people visited the museum to see the new designs and fabrics, but sadly all the garments were for export only, so English women had to be content to return to their coupons, dressmaking and 'make do and mend' policy as clothes rationing was to continue for several more years.

The clothes pictured on these pages are like those at the exhibition and represent the work of top London designers in 1946.

Try and find out more about the 'Britain Can Make It' exhibition. Draw pictures of some of the exhibits.

the 'country' look —
beaver corduroy
jacket and
herringbone tweed skirt

dinner dress
in black wool
crêpe

cocktail
dresses
in heavy
crêpe

tucked and
fitted grey
dinner dress

post-war beauty:
pink-rouged cheeks,
red lips and nails,
draped hair

The New Look, 1947-8

In 1947, Christian Dior, a French couturier, launched his revolutionary New Look to the fashion world. The new shape had unpadded, rounded shoulders, a shapely bustline, small waist and full skirts that reached well below the knee. It represented everything that women had missed during the austerity of the war years – colour, luxury and femininity – and it was an instant success.

Here is Audrey Somerville who is wearing some of the new fashions. On the right she has on a Christian Dior suit with a straw hat. It is a very feminine outfit compared to the square-shouldered jackets and straight knee-length skirts worn during the war years. Audrey has bought quite a few 'New Look' clothes and more items from her wardrobe are pictured on the opposite page. They include a barrel skirt, which is another of Dior's designs, and Audrey sometimes wears it as an alternative to the full, billowing skirts which feel so wonderful after the utility clothes of the last few years.

Not everyone praised these new fashions. Some people felt that it was wrong to use so much money and material on full skirts for rich women when others did not have enough to eat and rationing was still in force. In fact, when Dior first launched his new collection in Paris there were ugly scenes when women tore the dresses from the backs of some of the models and screamed: '40,000 francs for a dress and our children have no milk!' The British government even considered an emergency law to restrict the length of women's skirts as clothes were still rationed. However, the fashion world had been starved of change for so long that it needed an injection of new life and fresh ideas so the criticisms were soon buried under a tide of enthusiasm for the new styles.

intricately
draped
crêpe dress

fan-pleated
satin dress
worn with
velvet
beret

accessories

hat with
veil

safari hat

suit with
narrow barrel
skirt and
hipbone
pockets

high-heeled
sling-back
shoes

pleated
blouse

high-heeled
sandals

navy blue cloth
and calf sling-back
court shoes

37

The Post-War Men's Wardrobe, c. 1948

The fashionable line for men during the late 1940s was an exaggerated version of the late 1930s style of dress. Shoulders were broad but jackets tapered in to fit neatly around the hips, and trousers were quite wide and had turnups.

Here is Audrey's husband Richard who is wearing a formal dress suit. The jacket has long tails reaching below his knees and the trousers have silk braid along the outer leg seams. He always wears this suit with a stiff wing collar, and a white shirt, waistcoat and bow tie. For less formal occasions, Richard exchanges the dress coat for a dinner jacket and wears a soft collar in preference to the stiff wing collar.

Richard owns many suits, coats and jackets, some of which are shown on the opposite page. Some popular men's styles at this time have been inspired by service uniforms. An example of this is the wool jacket pictured in the centre. The belt and large pockets on this are reminiscent of a battle dress jacket.

Hats are still considered essential and Richard owns several different ones. Only two are shown here. The bowler is considered more formal than the soft felt trilby hat.

Richard's accessories include gloves, sticks, scarves, umbrellas and handkerchiefs.

c. 1948

three-piece
suit

overcoat,
check
trousers,
trilby hat

jacket with
military style
pockets and
belt

leather
gloves

leather shoes

suede
shoes

bowler
hat

maroon
velvet
smoking
jacket

Two Brides, c. 1949

It is now 1949 and Catherine Somerville's wedding day. Catherine has been a subaltern in the ATS but she has now left the forces and is going to marry a banker in the City of London.

She is very lucky because her parents have paid for a dressmaker to make her wedding gown for her. It is made of soft silk satin with a crêpe weave and the bodice fastens at the back with small self-covered buttons. The long sleeves are pointed at the wrists and slightly gathered into padded shoulders. The dress has a separate basque attached at the belt at the back and the skirt has a long full train. Her headdress is trimmed with flowers and she is carrying a pom-pom of flowers.

After their marriage Catherine and her husband will live in London.

Many brides had to make do without a wedding dress during the years immediately following the war. This was because wedding dresses were costly and they took many precious clothing coupons which could be better used for garments that could be worn more than once.

Here is Susan Adams who is also getting married. She has chosen to wear a New Look suit and matching coat in a light blue-grey worsted fabric. She is also wearing a white blouse, navy blue platform-soled shoes and a matching navy velvet hat with a veil. Susan had to surrender quite a few clothing coupons for her outfit but she does not mind as she can wear it on future occasions.

She made her blouse herself out of former RAF parachute material. This fabric is sold free of coupons and is relatively inexpensive so Susan has also made her petticoats and a night-dress from the same material. Ex-RAF fabric was usually white or lime green although occasionally orange could be obtained. Many young women used it to make dresses for their bridesmaids as other materials were in such short supply.

Susan is marrying an engineer. They will live together in a small house in a suburb of London.

Susan misses her friend Joan who married her American GI and now lives with him in the USA. The two girls write regularly to one another and always discuss the latest fashion news. See if you can find out anything about the American fashion industry at this time.

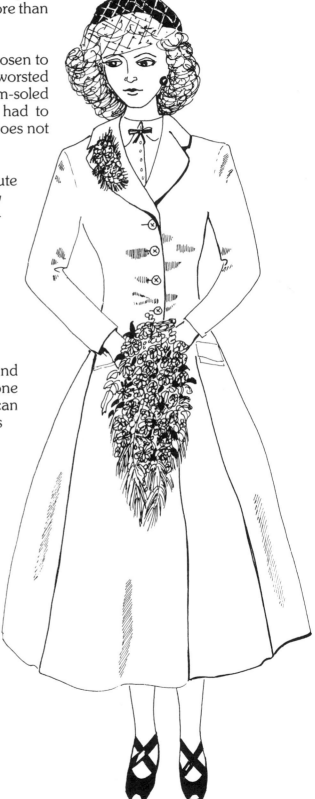

Female Fashions, c. 1951

In the early 1950s it was as if there was a longing to return to order and normality after the war. Women's fashions reflected this in smooth, elegant lines and classic coats and suits. Both pencil-slim skirts and the flared skirts of the New Look were popular for day wear, and for evening strapless gowns with bouffant skirts were frequently seen.

Great attention was given to accessories and 'what to wear with what' was a favourite theme in women's magazines. Gloves were worn with almost everything and so were hats until the mid-1950s when it became possible to be smart without one. Kerchiefs were sometimes worn around the shoulders and tied at the back, gypsy style, and artificial posies of flowers were often seen at the waist.

Good tailoring and good fabrics were considered most important and colours were often vivid and bright. Nylon was being used more and more for the manufacture of blouses, underwear and gloves, and women found it a great boon as it laundered so easily. Make-up was frequently vivid as many women like to paint their lips and nails bright red in imitation of the Hollywood stars.

Here is Catherine at her London home. Being married to a wealthy banker, she can afford the most fashionable clothes. Here she is wearing a slim, cream coloured suit in spun silk, which has a long stole emerging from the revers which falls across her shoulders and is tied at the back. It is lined with black taffeta.

Catherine's accessories are black and she wears her hair short in the popular 'urchin' cut.

More items from her wardrobe are pictured on the opposite page.

summer dress

beach dress with matching kerchief

a pencil-slim suit worn with a silk scarf and brooch

strapless evening dress with floral design

shoes

gloves and scarf

Male Fashions, c. 1953

This is Oliver Robertson, Catherine's husband, who works in the City of London. He is wearing a well-tailored overcoat, with a velvet collar and concealed front fastenings, under which he has on a three-piece suit. He is also wearing a bowler hat and is carrying his gloves and a rolled umbrella.

When Oliver is not working he dresses less formally. For example, he might wear a sports jacket and unmatching trousers and a soft flat cap instead of his bowler. For golf, he wears an outfit like that pictured opposite which consists of a cap, sports jacket, check shirt, knitted cardigan, plus fours, thick woollen socks and stout shoes. He also owns a duffle coat which he likes to wear on casual occasions. Duffle coats were first made in Duffel in Flanders in the eighteenth century. They became very popular in Britain after World War II because their thick tufted nap made them very warm. They were usually camel, navy or grey in colour.

Oliver's suits usually have matching waistcoats but sometimes he wears a bright contrasting one as a change from the more sombre colours of his working suits. His other casual clothes include several knitted cardigans, sweaters and pullovers and some suede shoes rather than the more usual leather ones.

Oliver wears his hair short and is clean shaven.

duffle coat

suede shoes

shoes and scarf

golfing outfit

blazer

waistcoat

gloves

45

Summer Leisure, c. 1954

It is a beautiful summer day and Catherine and Oliver have invited some friends and family to their home for drinks and a game of tennis. On this page, Catherine (seated), her young sister Elizabeth and Oliver are watching some of the activity.

Catherine is wearing an off-the-shoulder striped cotton top with striped three-quarter length slacks. She has rope-soled sandals on her feet, a straw sunhat on her head and she is holding her sunglasses. Elizabeth is wearing a matching short-sleeved shirt and shorts in brightly patterned cotton fabric. She has her hair in a pony tail, a style which is very popular with young people. Oliver has on a light blue cotton shirt which he is wearing over a pair of dark blue shorts, and he has tennis shoes on his feet.

Jane and James, the twins whom you last saw on page 12, are all ready for a game of tennis. Men's tennis outfits have changed very little during recent years, and James is wearing a white sweater over a white T-shirt and shorts, white ankle socks and tennis shoes. Jane's tennis dress is a fashionable 'A' line shape and is made of Terylene which means that the pleats stay nicely in place. She is also wearing white ankle socks and tennis shoes and she has a scarf tied around her head.

The 1950s signalled the beginning of a more relaxed attitude to clothes. More and more people were taking up sport and leisure activities which created a demand for fashionable yet comfortable clothes like these.

An Engineer and his Wife, c. 1955

We will now return to Susan and her husband Jim who live in a suburb of London with their two small children.

Jim is an engineer and as he earns a moderately good salary he can afford to run a car and buy nice clothes for himself and his family. Here he is wearing a casual outfit consisting of a sports jacket, an open-necked cotton shirt, trousers and lace-up shoes.

Susan is wearing a white blouse and a fashionable American-style dirndl skirt. This is a very full skirt which must be supported by stiff petticoats in order to make it stand out. Some young women wear petticoats with wiring in them (reminiscent of the crinoline of the 1850s!), but Susan prefers stiff nylon or nylon net. It is also fashionable to have a large bosom due to a trend set by the Hollywood movie stars of the 1940s and early 1950s. The most popular bra is the 'sweater girl' bra, the aim of which is to create an exaggerated high pointed bosom by means of stitching and padding. Susan wears one of these. If she and Jim go out for the evening however, she will probably wear a strapless bra with an evening dress.

Susan does not go to work any more as she prefers to spend time at home with her children. She makes many of their clothes herself but she frequently takes them to one of the large department stores to buy garments for them.

The 1950s were years of great expansion for large department stores like Marks and Spencer and the British Home Stores. See if you can find out more about them and the kinds of clothes that they stocked.

waist slip in
nylon

long-line strapless
bra

nylon bra with
wide, pointed circle -
stitched cups –
a 'sweater girl' bra

Young Fashion, c. 1955

Susan always enjoys a visit from her young sister Alice. They spend many happy evenings together, sometimes remembering the years they enjoyed at Mr Westlake's farm during the war. In the summer, if the weather is nice, they go out shopping on Susan's motor scooter. In the picture, Susan and Alice are both wearing light cotton dresses as it is a very hot day. Susan also has on black leather gloves for driving and low-heeled court shoes. Alice is wearing light leather pumps instead of shoes. Neither Susan nor Alice are wearing crash helmets, as this was not required by law in the 1950s as it is now.

Alice is working as a fashion model so she always wears the latest style in clothes. She is particularly fond of baggy sweaters, a style that originated in Italy and is now very popular in Britain. She usually wears them with tight trousers which end above the ankle and, of course, a sweater girl bra! Alice also enjoys wearing jeans which she might team up with a knitted twin set. Original Levi jeans were first made in the USA for the gold rush miners in 1850 and they remained popular with labourers. In the early 1950s they became fashionable with college students and later with just about everyone else!

Think about Alice's freedom both in terms of her mobility and in the clothes she wears. How does her lifestyle compare with that of her mother when she was young?

Teddy Boys and Rock and Roll, c. 1955

One of the most interesting features of the 1950s was the rise of the 'young generation'. Young people were frequently economically independent and between leaving school and getting married they enjoyed the luxury of a freedom that their parents had never known. They went to dances, clubs and cafés and listened to their own kind of music. They wore clothes peculiar to their age group and department stores began setting up special teenage boutiques. It was as if there was a revolt against the established order and the younger generation no longer looked to their elders for a lead, wanting their own style instead.

The Teddy boy movement was one example of this. It began in London's East End in the early 1950s and by 1956 could be seen all around Britain. The characteristic features of the Teddy boy style of dress were a long jacket with padded shoulders, trousers with straight and narrow legs, narrow ties, fluorescent socks and large, crêpe-soled shoes called 'creepers'. Hair was arranged in a 'duck's arse' style which meant that it was cut with a long quiff at the front and slicked back with grease. It was essentially a tough look and many Teddy boys formed gangs and were frequently seen loitering on street corners or in 'caffs' waiting to pick up girls.

This is Alice's brother Alan, who is an electrician. He likes to dress in the Teddy boy style although he does not belong to a gang. Instead he likes to go to dances or to spend evenings with a few friends in his favourite café listening to the juke box.

maroon leather laced
shoe – Teddy boy wear

Alice loves going to dances and enjoys doing the 'rock and roll' with her boyfriend for which she wears very full skirts and layers of petticoats. In this picture she is wearing a cotton print dress with a dirndl skirt, a short matching jacket and high-heeled court shoes.

Find out more about rock and roll in the 1950s and some of the famous stars like Bill Haley and the Comets, Elvis Presley, Buddy Holly and the Everly Brothers. What kind of clothes did they wear?

A Day at the Seaside, c. 1956

Peter Black (whom you last saw as a boy on page 17) also lives and works in London. He is married to Sandra and they have two small children, Gillian and Christopher. Peter is a stallholder in a street market so he does not earn a great deal of money. However, he likes to spend as much time as possible with his family and occasionally they all take the train and have a day out, either in the country or at the seaside.

Here you can see them enjoying themselves on the beach. Sandra does a lot of dress-making and knitting for herself and the children in order to save money on clothes. In the picture she is wearing a cardigan with a zip front, a floral print cotton dress that she has made herself and leather sandals. Christopher and Gillian are both wearing T-shirts, shorts and canvas shoes. Gillian's shorts have been knitted by hand and have a bib front.

Although on the beach, Peter is wearing the same sports jacket that he wears to work as he does not have any real casual clothes. He also has on a cotton shirt, trousers with turnups and leather sandals. When Peter is at work he wears a cloth cap and an overcoat or raincoat over his jacket and trousers as it is frequently very cold at the market. Draw a picture of him at his stall talking to some of his customers. What might they be wearing?

Holidays at the seaside became very popular in the 1950s. Holiday camps like Butlins had become big business and attracted many people. Find out more about them. Are they different today?

A Fashion Model, c. 1958

It is now 1958 and we will return to Alice, who has become quite a successful model. During the last three years she has modelled many beautiful clothes designed by famous couturiers and as she is earning a good salary she can afford to buy the latest fashions for her own wardrobe. On these pages you can see some of the outfits that have been her favourites.

Christian Dior was the first couturier to christen each of his collections with a theme name. In 1955 he launched his 'A' line in which the clothes had narrow shoulders and slightly fitted waistlines gradually widening to the hips. On this page Alice is wearing an 'A' line dress in off-white with navy shoes and gloves. Dior was very particular about his hats and this one has been chosen to compliment the line of the dress. See if you can find out about Dior's 'H' line and some of his other famous designs.

On the opposite page Alice is wearing clothes from her own wardrobe. She now wears her hair slightly longer in a softer style and her accessories and make up are always chosen with care so that she appears well groomed at all times.

'A' line, 1955

1957
camel hair coat
worn over
calf-length
skirt

1956
chunky knitted
pullover with ankle-length
tweed slacks

1958
tweed suit,
jacket has
bloused back

Conclusion, c. 1960

Now we come to 1960 and to the end of our period. Here are Catherine and Oliver with their daughter Clare who is now 11.

Catherine is wearing a suit with a straight skirt and a jacket which is collarless and has three-quarter length sleeves (a style which is to become very popular in the 1960s). Her shoes have stiletto heels and she is carrying her hat, gloves and handbag.

Oliver is wearing a casual outfit which consists of a blazer-style jacket in knitted cotton, a white shirt, cotton trousers and slip-on shoes.

Clare is already interested in fashion and as more shops are now catering for young people there are many different styles to choose from when Catherine and Oliver buy her clothes. She is wearing a mohair top, linen trousers and boots and she has arranged her hair in two bunches.

As we leave Catherine and her family, think about how fashions have changed during the 20 years covered by this book. We began in 1940 at a time of restrictions and austerity, and end in 1960 at a time of freedom and relative prosperity. Clothes are now more easily available and there is a greater variety of styles and fabrics for men, women and children. Think also about the social upheaval that has taken place. How has it affected fashion? Finally, try to see the relationship between costume and the context in which it is worn. How do people's lifestyles and occupations affect the clothes they choose to wear?

Glossary

'A' line	a Christian Dior design for women in which clothes are narrow at the shoulders and wider at the hips (*pages 49, 58*)
auxiliary	someone who is helpful (*page 24*)
basque	a continuation of the bodice below the waist (*page 40*)
bolero	a woman's short jacket (*page 23*)
bouffant	puffed up, as applied to hairstyles or skirts (*page 42*)
box coat	a boxy-shaped woman's coat with padded square shoulders and a loose fit around the waist (*page 21*)
Brilliantine	hair grease which fixes hair in position and gives a shiny effect (*page 8*)
breeches	short trousers fastened below the knee (*pages 26, 27, 28*)
couture	dress making
creepers	thick, crêpe-soled shoes worn by Teddy boys (*page 54*)
dirndl skirt	a full skirt, gathered at the waist (*pages 51, 55*)
duck's arse	a haircut, popular with Teddy boys, which has a long quiff at the front and is slicked back with grease (*page 54*)
duffle coat	a loose-fitting hooded coat with toggle fastenings made from thick woollen cloth with a nap (*page 45*)
guaging	gathering with parallel rows of stitches (rather like smocking) (*page 22*)
haute couture	the design and making of fashionable clothes
jodpurs	riding breeches which are full to the knee then tight to the ankle (*page 9*)
kerchief	a decorative shawl (*page 43*)
khaki	a fabric of twilled cotton or wool (*pages 18, 24, 30*)
lisle	fine, hard-twisted thread (*page 24*)
nap	the surface given to a cloth by raising and then cutting and smoothing the short fibres (*page 44*)
pinafore dress	a sleeveless dress with a bib front worn over a blouse or jumper (*page 23*)
plus fours	men's baggy knee breeches, ending just below the knees (*page 45*)
pumps	flat shoes with soft, low cut uppers (*page 53*)
revers	the turned-back edges of a coat or waistcoat (*page 42*)
serge	durable twilled worsted fabric suitable for hard wear (*page 18*)
siren suit	combined jacket and trouser suit in a warm material (*page 15*)
slipover	a sleeveless jumper (*pages 12, 17*)
slit trench	a two-man trench which provides short-term shelter and protection for soldiers (*page 19*)
subaltern	an officer below the rank of captain (*page 40*)
Terylene	the trade name for the polyester fibre discovered in 1941 (*page 49*)
worsted	woollen yarn (*pages 11, 41*)

Book List

Black, J.A. & Garland, M.A.	*A History of Fashion*, 2nd ed., Orbis Publishing, 1980
Boucher, François	*A History of Costume in the West*, new ed., Thames and Hudson, 1987
Bradfield, N.	*Historical Costumes of England 1066-1956*, 2nd ed., Harrap, 1958
Byrde, Penelope	*A Visual History of Costume in the 20th Century*, Batsford, 1986
Canter Cremers-van der Does, Eline	*The Agony of Fashion*, Blandford Press, 1980
Contini, Mila	*Fashion from Ancient Egypt to the Present Day*, Hamlyn, 1965
Cox, Mary	*British Women at War*, John Murray, 1941
Cunnington, C.W. and P.	*History of Underclothes*, revised ed., Faber & Faber, 1981
Cunnington, P. and Mansfield, A.	*A Handbook of Costume in the 20th Century 1900-1950*, Faber & Faber, 1973

Dorner, Jane	*Fashion*, Octopus Books, 1974
Dorner, Jane	*Fashion in the Forties and Fifties*, Ian Allan, 1975
Ewing, E.	*Dress and Undress*, Batsford, 1977
Ewing, E.	*Fashion in Underwear*, Batsford, 1971
Ewing, E.	*History of Children's Costume*, Batsford, 1977
Ewing, E.	*History of 20th Century Fashion*, Batsford, 1974
Ewing, E.	*Women in Uniform*, Batsford, 1975
Foster, V.	*Bags and Purses*, Batsford, 1982
Gaisford, John (ed.)	*Times Gone By – a photographic record of Britain 1856-1956*, Marshall Cavendish, 1985
Garland, Madge	*Fashion*, Penguin, 1962
Goldsmith, M. and Glynn, Prudence	*In Fashion – Dress in the 20th Century*, George Allen & Unwin Ltd, 1978
Hall, Carolyn	*The Forties in Vogue*, Octopus Books, 1985
Hansen, Henry Harold	*Costume Cavalcade*, Methuen, 1956
Hillier, Bevis	*The Style of the Century 1900-1980*, Herbert Press, 1983
Howell, Georgina	*In Vogue – six decades of fashion*, Allen Lane, 1975
Keenan, B.	*Dior in Vogue*, Octopus Books, 1981
Lansdell, Avril	*Wedding Fashions 1860-1980*, Shire Publications Ltd, 1983
Laver, James	*Costume and Fashion: a concise history*, 2nd ed., Thames and Hudson, 1982
Mollo, A.	*Army Uniforms of World War II*, Blandford Press, 1973
Peacock, John	*Fashion Sketchbook, 1920-1960*, Thames and Hudson, 1977
Robinson, Julian	*Fashion in the Forties*, Academy Editions, 2nd Imp., 1980
Sichel, Marion	*Costume Reference Series, No 9: 1939-1950*, Batsford, 1979
Stevenson, Pauline	*Bridal Fashions*, Ian Allan Ltd, 1978
Sunderland Echo	*Canny add Sunlun*, Portsmouth and Sunderland Newspapers PLC, 1983
Swann, June	*Costume Accessories Series, Shoes*, Batsford, 1982
Victoria and Albert Museum	*400 years of Fashion*, 1984
White, Palmer	*Elsa Schiaparelli*, Aurum Press, 1986
Windrow, M. & Hook, R.	*The Footsoldier*, OUP, 1982
Yass, Marion	*The Home Front 1939-1945*, Wayland, 1971

Places to Visit

Here are a few ideas for some interesting places to visit which will help you with your study of costume in the 1940s and 1950s.

Bath Museum of Costume, Assembly Rooms, Bath, Avon.

Bethnal Green Museum of Childhood (a branch of the Victoria and Albert Museum).

Gallery of English Costume, Platt Hall, Platt Fields, Rusholme, Manchester M14 5LL.

Imperial War Museum, Lambeth Road, London SE1 6HZ.

Museum of London, London Wall, London EC2Y 5HN.

National Army Museum, Royal Hospital Road, London, SW3 4HT.

Victoria and Albert Museum, Cromwell Road, South Kensington, London SW7 2RL.

Also visit your local museum and find out if they have any items of clothing from this period that you could look at.

Things to Do

1. Find out if any of your relatives remember World War II. Ask them about their memories and what kind of clothes they wore. See if they have any photographs for you to look at.

2. Try designing some clothes that take a minimum amount of material, just as fashion designers had to do during the war. What would you do if you had to 'Make Do and Mend'? (page 22)

3. Find out more about soldiers' uniforms in World War II. Draw pictures of them.

4. Go to your local library and look up any books on shops and shopping. Find out about what shops, particularly department stores, were like during this period.

5. Find out all you can about the production of man-made fabrics during the 1940s and 1950s.

6. Look at the life stories of these three famous designers: Christian Dior (French), Norman Hartnell (British), and Main R. Bocher (American). Draw some of the styles that they created.

7. Do a project on the 'Young Revolution' of the 1950s. Include Rock and Roll, Teddy boys and the new teenage fashions.

8. Do a project on 'Shoes' in the 1940s and 1950s. Find out all about the many different styles, for example the 'creepers' worn by Teddy boys and the stiletto heels that came from Italy. Also, see if you can find out about the work of Salvatore Ferragamo, the famous Italian shoe designer.

c. 1955